A Cellist's Guide
to
THE NEW APPROACH

A Cellist's Guide

to
THE NEW APPROACH

by
Claude Kenneson

With a Foreword by
Kato Havas

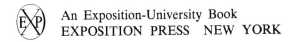

An Exposition-University Book
EXPOSITION PRESS   NEW YORK

To Horace Britt in Gratitude

First Edition

©1974 by Claude Kenneson

Library of Congress Catalog Card Number: 73-86546

ISBN 0-682-47819-9

Manufactured in the United States of America

Contents

—

Foreword

When teaching, like playing, is realised in the framework of creative art, it ceases to be a profession. It becomes a vocation, a new way of life, a never-ending study of the fathomless potential in each individual. And the necessity to release physical tensions and mental anxieties in the pupil becomes an essential prerequisite. However, this cannot be achieved through a clarity of purpose alone. It needs boundless compassion, imagination and constant fluidity of thought. Claude Kenneson has all these attributes.

There are many good teachers and quite a number of first-rate teachers. But there are only a few great ones. Professor Kenneson is certainly among these.

I consider it a privilege that he has adapted The New Approach to Violin Playing to his "Cellist's Guide." It is done with great understanding and insight. This book will certainly make an important contribution to the art of teaching.

Kato Havas

Introduction

When pedagogical innovations occur in the musical world, controversy invariably arises as the new ideas are related to existing traditions. Once such innovations prove to be valid, the disquiet that comes from facing the unknown usually subsides, and the new procedures are accepted and used to musical advantage. Several decades ago, inquiring string players were coming to grips with the principles being taught by D. C. Dounis. Because his ideas seemed a radical departure from the norm, his work was viewed with a certain wariness. However, it is interesting to note that, along with violinists and violists, several cellists sought information and instruction from this source, realizing that there was more in common between the playing of the various stringed instruments than met the attention of the casual observer. Whether or not the Dounis principles are universally accepted, the fact is that significant cello playing has been formed on the basis of his teachings, and the ideas are being used frequently and with recognized success.

In her book *A New Approach to Violin Playing,* Kato Havas remarks, "It is not a question of teaching and imposing a certain dogma, but of making it possible for the student to 'let it happen.' From the very first lesson, the student is trained how to differentiate between causes and effects. This New Approach, through the compelling logic of certain basic play actions, is based on the idea of balance, not of strength. There are no 'mechanical' finger exercises as we understand them. The aim of the exercises is not a strengthening process but an elimination, through finding the exact balance, of all conscious muscular action save one, so that the mind can be freed from the impossible task of concentrating on two or more things at once. Then if this one conscious muscular action is properly developed, it is able to transmit and control the musical and artistic impulses of the player to such an extent that all mechanical problems disappear and there is

9

nothing left for him to do but to give full vent to his imagination."[1]

One can only fully appreciate the value of what Miss Havas has to say about playing music when one has accepted and understood the concepts of the New Approach and actually begun to explore it in the context of one's own playing. As I observed this application of the New Approach to my own playing, I realized that here was a new possibility for *all* string players who wish to gain control in their playing and to use their communicative powers to the fullest extent. The reader should understand that I have not attempted to impose a violin playing "method" on the art of cello playing. Kato Havas' New Approach is not a "method" in the general sense, but a meaningful organization of thought processes which focuses the mental concentration on a musical idea, the physical realization of that idea coming from a logically-conceived use of the body's natural balances. The New Approach is an approach to tone production, and is an enormously strong force which moulds one's musical thoughts and physical prowess into a unified performing experience.

The concepts of tone production which Kato Havas understood when creating her *New Approach to Violin Playing* are frequently exemplified in cellistic performance by players whose natural instincts allow them the constant use of the natural balances, and whose musicality predominates over technical procedures. What better illustrates these concepts than the eloquent sounds produced by Pablo Casals' performance of the *Sarabande* from the C Minor Suite by Bach? With its strong linear progression of intervals, and its simplicity of design, this music has a certain profundity in Casals' performance because the very essence of this playing is the rhythmic vocalization of the melodic line.

Miss Havas has meaningful answers to the probing questions of her students, and I thank her for her revelations. During my initial consultation with Miss Havas about the principles of the

---

[1]Kato Havas, *A New Approach to Violin Playing* (London: Bosworth and Co. Ltd., 1961), p. 2.

New Approach, we spoke of many things which influence the cellist, such as the application of the simple laws governing the use of the natural balances, performance attitudes that are free from undue tension and anxiety, and the mental-physical approach to tone production and hence to music-making that creates an artistic reflection of one's musical concepts.

To the player familiar only with orthodox traditional "methods," the directness and utter simplicity of Miss Havas' New Approach may prove disarming. She has in her own teaching organized the common tendencies of many players (regardless of their technical advancement) into a body of information which is balanced by an organization of solutions arrived at through the use of the New Approach principles. Following this practice, I have attempted to do the same for the cellists.

Kato Havas has written, "No one can learn to ride a bicycle from a set of written instructions, and this book *A New Approach to Violin Playing* does not of course presume to teach a student to play the violin." Likewise my book does not attempt by a set of exercises to teach anyone to play the cello, but it was my desire to introduce to cellists the New Approach, a disciplined training based on our common need to cope with the desire to move.

Throughout the ensuing pages, I shall occasionally draw the reader's attention to certain *tendencies* that have been observed in the playing of cellists of widely varying levels of physical accomplishment. I have selected these specific aspects to set apart as tendencies because I consider them common to the playing experience, arising as they do from our physical response to touching the instrument and bow at the points of contact. Generations of cellists have grappled with these tendencies, seeking solution to their immobility through the avenue of orthodox practices. These practices often offer no solution other than "exercises" intended to break through immobility with sheer strength. After stating the tendency, I have offered another observation which I consider to be the "New Approach point of view" concerning the counteraction of such tendencies, and I have called these observations *solutions*.

This knowledge has been gained empirically, and I offer the tendency-solution sections of the book with the hope that these sections will serve as a point of departure for further investigation by all cellists interested in these matters. Perhaps the message in this book will arouse the spirit of inquiry in cellists and lead them to an examination of the biomechanical and neurophysiological rationale of the New Approach. The noted biological scientist Dr. F. A. Hellebrandt has written a significant series of articles recently published in *The Strad* which illuminates the principles and practices of the New Approach with scientific explanation of the fundamental teaching devices. The discussion is limited to *what* is done and *why* it is successful. The study of these papers will help the cellist gain insight into the New Approach principles as he learns that the pedagogical devices are used as a means to connote a biological phenomenon which can be explained and understood in the light of modern neurophysiological thought. That which is taught by Kato Havas is here clearly supported by unadorned scientific fact garnered from a vast body of knowledge which offers indestructible scientific basis for the New Approach philosophy, principles and practices.

Acknowledgments

I am grateful to both the University of Alberta and the Canada Council for their assistance through research grants which made possible my initial consultations with Kato Havas. I wish to thank my colleagues Professor Abraham Chavez of the University of Colorado and Dr. Frances A. Hellebrandt, Professor Emeritus of the University of Wisconsin, for their critical opinion of the manuscript of this book. I wish to express my gratitude to Mr. Brian Harris, Lecturer in music history at the University of Alberta, for his patient editing of the text throughout its development, and Mr. Wille Rauschning for his excellent photographs of my pupil and graduate assistant, Mr. Peter Rudolfi. I am indebted to my many pupils in both North America and Great Britain for their mounting interest in the advancement of the New Approach, to Mrs. Flore Shaw for her deep understanding and personal support of my educational ideals, and, of course, to Kato Havas, whose genius has given us all a new insight into the performance experience.

A Cellist's Guide
to
THE NEW APPROACH

"Only this impulse coming from the centre of the body instead of each extremity . . . rather like an image of what I feel at the time . . . will group the different movements in a unified whole."

PABLO CASALS

1 The Fundamental Balances

The New Approach leads to an organized way of dealing with our desire to move. It helps one break through the barriers of tension and immobility. However, before one proceeds to this investigation of movement in cello playing, thought must be given to the sitting posture and the natural holding of the instrument and bow.

RECEIVING THE CELLO

In earlier periods, it seemed necessary to clutch the cello between the knees, resting it heavily on the calves of the legs. With many players this position must have inhibited body movement. The early cellists were simply following the habits of the gamba players who did not use an endpin to support the instrument. It was not until the nineteenth century that the Belgian cellist François Servais became a champion of the endpin. From that period to the present, the adjustability of both the height and the angle of the cello has led to improved methods of holding the instrument. An increasing effort is being made by some modern players to rid themselves of excessive contact with the instrument. The left hand must merge with the fingerboard, and the bow must cling to the vibrating string while the body lightly touches the cello, creating an elastic bond.

No cellist should be committed to physical discomfort. When one speaks of "holding the cello," he is actually referring to relating the instrument to the body in a most natural way. The cello must be supported by a properly-chosen endpin that keeps its contact with the floor, never slipping out of place.

POSITIONAL SUBSTRATE

The cellist should sit upon a flat-bottomed chair. Chairs with contoured bottoms tend to force the cellist's body into a fixed

position, and most often this position is not one that is appropriate to cello playing. The player sits on the edge of the chair and leans forward, plants his feet firmly on the floor, and *receives* the instrument by taking it gently between the legs and allowing its back to rest lightly against the chest.

The successful use of the body's natural repertoire of movement depends to a great degree on the player's attitude toward the exploration of this sitting posture. The player moves away from the self-learning processes of the New Approach when he fits himself to the cello in order to fulfill a postural attitude pictured in a "method" book, or imitates the visual appearance of another player. The first step is to be aware of *one's own natural way of sitting,* then to develop an attitude of dynamic exploration so that with each playing experience this posture is attained. The posture is never static. It is always resilient and flexible.

Sitting on the edge of the chair and leaning forward, the cellist should tilt the pelvis so that the weight of the body rests squarely on the tuberosities. As the player seeks this fundamental balance, he will know best when he has found the most desirable posture—the sitting position most natural to his own body. When the weight has been placed in this way, not only will the torso feel balanced over its center of gravity, but the legs will open naturally to accept the cello. It is into this positional substrate that the cello is placed. One does not fit the body to the cello, but allows the cello to fit into this sitting posture found through seeking the fundamental balance.

The cello by its very structural nature lends itself to proper placement once the natural sitting posture has been found through exploration. When the cello is thus placed, it can be held with ease and naturalness as long as the chair height and the endpin adjustment have been given careful consideration. After the first few contacts with the instrument, the cellist will know that finding this posture is a matter of *doing* and not of theorizing. He must become deeply involved with the matter of his own self-learning. Through a trial and error system of moving to seek the feelings of comfort and naturalness, he will find the fundamental balances which promote the full use of the body's potential for mobility.

HOLDING THE BOW: THE RIGHT THUMB

In this century, the idea has been accepted by many players that the bow hand should retain a form similar to that observed when one allows the right arm to hang relaxed by the side. In this attitude, the thumb will relate itself to the second and third fingers, and a natural arching of all the fingers will take place. When the tip of the thumb is placed against the second finger, it will touch the middle phalange of this finger, creating a loose and natural circle. When the bow is inserted into a relaxed hand, it is into this circle that it fits.

Once the tip of the thumb is in proper contact with the bow stick, one should flex the thumb joint, rolling the bow between the fingers until the bow hair comes to the thumb and touches it. In this exercise the player must be certain that the hair is brought to the thumb in this rolling action. The thumb must not be pushed forward to contact the hair. When the thumb is bent, the large muscles which attach it to the hand will relax, and the wrist will be unlocked and able to move in all directions. The bent thumb also encourages the natural arching of all the fingers. When the thumb is placed in this way, it may come into contact with both the bow stick and the bow hair. It is the only one of the fingers to be so engaged. The right thumb is one of the strongest, yet most flexible and resilient agents used in holding the bow.

When the bent thumb is in position, the four fingers simply fall over the stick and rest on it. There will be no gripping with the fingers if the endpads of the fingertips can be. released at will. There should be a strong impression of contact between the top of the bow stick and the underside of the fingers (in the area of the middle phalanges). There should be no "space" between the stick and these phalanges. With this manner of holding the bow, one learns to accept the fact that the cello *will* support the bow; the bow is neither pinched nor gripped with

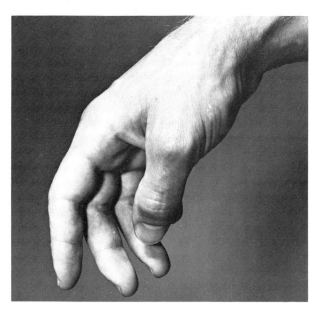

The relaxed hand

The circle

The bow inserted

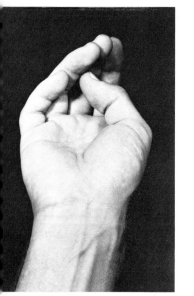

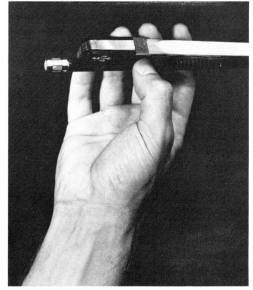

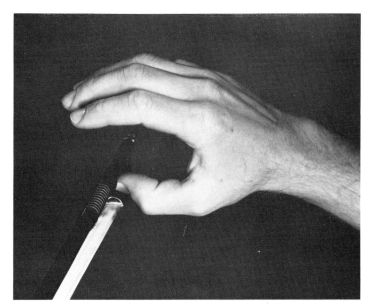

The bow balanced on the thumb

The fingers dropped over

The endpads released

the fingertips. The control from the bent thumb which can produce no downward pressure is valuable. To make certain that the fingers are not gripping the bow, simply anchor the tip of the thumb, remember that the instrument holds the bow (supports it), rest against it, and flip up the fingers at will to reassure that the bow is controlled from underneath by the thumb.

TENDENCY   To clutch the bow with the fingertips, manipulating it, lifting to decrease the weight on the string at the frog, and pressing to increase the weight at the tip.

SOLUTION   To control the bow from underneath by the thumb which is bent and may be in contact with both the stick and the bow hair. Drop the fingers onto the stick and release the endpads.

THE "CHECK POINTS"

From the outset of each association with the instrument, the cellist must search for the postural position that allows the body to function with all its potential for making music on the cello. This natural position of the body automatically provides an elegant substrate for a delicately mobile arm suspension. In this naturally-evolved situation, the player does not concern himself with learning a set of new exercises to suspend the bow arm. On the contrary, the posture allows the player to immediately use a physical reality that nature has provided.

The initial reaction to the bow hold may be one of clutching or gripping. The bow itself is a hard object, and at the point of contact, the fingertips may respond to this hardness. Once the use of the bow as a musical tool is perceived, the player's attitude toward the bow hold will be greatly influenced. Here a comparison can be drawn between the use of the bow and the use of a walking stick or probe. In his book *The Tacit Dimension*[1] Michael Polanyi has explained that when using a walking stick for the first time, the impact against the fingers and palm will be felt. But as one learns to use the stick for feeling one's way, the awareness of its impact on the hand is transformed into a sense of its point touching the objects that are being explored. This is how an interpretative effort transposes meaningless feelings into meaningful ones, and places these at some distance from the original feeling.

So it is with the bow. Once the player experiences the reality of drawing forth a musical tone with this tool, he becomes acutely aware of the contact between the bow and the string and only tacitly aware of the bow hold itself. The feeling of impact between the fingers and the bowstick is transformed into a sense of the tone-producing action taking place far away from the hand where the hair touches the vibrating string. The vibrations coursing through the stick and hair constantly relay information back to the nervous system through the sensitively touching hand.

If the player uses isolated movements in the hand and forces the pressure onto the bow stick, locking the small joints of the

---

[1]Michael Polanyi, *The Tacit Dimension* (New York: Doubleday and Co. Ltd., 1966), p. 12.

fingers into a state of immobility, all the bowing exercises created by the great masters of the past will not give the ultimate sense of ease to the bowing, or allow the cellist to use his real power through balance and resilience. Once the player is put in the unfortunate position of being immobile, tension will gather and movement will be frustrated.

When the bow arm is suspended the entire right-arm unit will feel weightless, and this is an ideal sensation for the cellist to deal with when making music. Once the arm is suspended, consider the mobility of these three major check points: *the shoulder joint, the elbow and the wrist.* One should be able to move these joints at will while the arm unit is suspended in the playing position with the bow resting on the strings. The movement of these checkpoints will display their free action and will dispel any tension. It is in the area of these three major checkpoints that tensions gather during playing. By moving these joints, tension is dispelled. To release tensions, one needs only to move!

TENDENCY   To lift the hand into position and hold the bow tightly by the fingertips.

SOLUTION   To feel the entire arm unit dropped into place from above the playing position. The suspended arm allows the hand to hold the bow sensitively, picking up the vibrations of the tone production as they occur between the hair and the string.

ISOMETRIC CONTRACTIONS

Gripping with the fingers stiffens every successive joint moving from the periphery to the most proximal joint. When one observes a player whose bowing apparatus is characterized by locked, rigid joints, it is worth considering why the joints are locked and what effects this immobility has on his performance. Rigidity in any one of the check points indicates the desire to apply a pressure in a nearby area. In the case of many cellists, it would seem that a sense of strength or power is evoked by contraction without movement. One is sometimes tempted to physically reproduce certain images of stillness, to pose in portrait-like positions. When the player is not fulfilling his music-making goals through a naturally-moving body—not acting out his musical conception with moving physical gestures—his thoughts may well turn to notions of security through stillness. The perfection of a still pose is far removed from the exigencies of musical performance on the cello. Isometric contractions, those muscular contractions without movement, coupled with the feelings of hardness at the points of contact between body and tool, will prove barriers to the player. As the player learns to use the spontaneous reactions of his body in cello playing, far greater power will be achieved through the use of natural balance and movement. Cellists must leave behind all thoughts of applying localized pressure—force—as it leads to immobility.

TENDENCY   To apply localized and isolated pressure at various points in the bowing arm.

SOLUTION   To free the joints by moving them so that tension is dispelled and weight is redistributed through movement. One should let the power flow from proximal point to distal point with no obstacles in its path, and, in this sense, should play from the "inside outward."

EXPLORATION OF FEELING

If the bow arm hangs suspended, the hand will seem to "float," and the player will not concern himself with the sensation of hand weight. The point of contact between the bow and the string is only an effect of the balanced arm, and one must constantly search for the right point of resistance in the string. The cellist must be constantly involved in an *exploration of feeling* for the appropriate point of contact that will reproduce the musical concept held in his mind. One soon learns through this experimentation with movement that various levels of dynamics are produced by different placements of the point of contact between bow and string. The measurement is achieved through searching for a feeling of resistance in the string to the weight of the bow.

In the course of playing, the bow hold itself will not be a point of conscious attention. On the contrary, the connection between bow hair and string will send vibrations to the hand which transform the holding sensation. The mind can be freed from concentrating and directing the holding action itself. The sensing of the contact between bow hair and string will constantly transmit information back to the nervous system, keeping the body oriented to the music-making and working spontaneously.

2 The Gestures

When playing music on the cello, the player acts out the musical conceptions held in his mind through a series of physical gestures. These gestures are at the same time natural and cellistic. They are *natural* because they evolve from the body's normal repertoire of movements. They are *cellistic* because they function in such a way as to transform musical concepts into sound when they activate the instrument.

THE BOWING ARC

The movements of the bow follow the *path of an arc*. If one allows the bow to travel on a path where the suspended arm naturally takes it, the arc can be easily observed. One does not create the bowing arc. The arc evolves naturally from the positional substrate that provides an elegantly mobile arm suspension. The arc curves in the direction *opposite* to the curvature of the bridge. When an angular movement is made with the bow, the movement either tends to wither and stop at the ends of the stroke, or it may be abrupt, even violent, and go against the nature of the rhythmic flow of the musical ideas. Without the use of the bowing arc, isolated movements of the hands and fingers are needed to change the direction of the bow strokes.

CHANGE OF DIRECTION

To change direction, simply slide down the lip of the arc, and in doing this gain new momentum. When the change of direction is accomplished in this way, the bowing is self-propelled. Once the movement is triggered, the impetus carries the arm with little or no further contraction until the end of the arc is approached. The muscular activity involved in the change of direction is to a great degree self-controlling. When the bow is guided from underneath by the bent thumb, it seems to be much longer than it actually is. To establish a natural movement of the bow over the path of this arc, one should use the advantages of

31

The path of the arc

a loose and pliable thumb guiding the bow in this self-propelled manner. The bow movement can soon be forgotten at the conscious level and can become involuntary.

OPEN-STRING PRACTICE

During the open-string practice, the cellist can put into action many elements of the technique. The controls that bring beauty to the playing of open strings are the same controls that bring beauty to any composition in the repertoire. One must create a vivid mental image of the tone. The tone must be imbued with all the necessary musical attributes. This will set the goal for the physical movement.

Mechanical exercises unrelated to musical ideas have no place in the training of the cellist. The musical progress of the player may be impeded if he allows musically-undirected exercising to become a habit during his practicing. Every sound, without exception, must be directed according to its musical meaning. With the open-string playing, the mind must immediately be concerned with the quality and duration of the note, and, when two or more notes are played, with the musical relationship of interval progressions. In this way one sets the habit of putting the focus of concentration where it belongs—on the musical concepts, and not on the particulars of the technique. Once the body is triggered to move, the cellist must simply search for balance. The body with its ancient memory of balance will redistribute its parts so that the center of gravity always remains within the limits of the base of support. This happens *automatically* without any direction by the mind.

During the entire process of performing the basic strokes on the open strings, the cellist must demand ease and comfort in the movement. As the heavier muscles take on the work of this basic stroke, the forearm is lightened. One never need fear having too much weight on the bow as long as it is in motion. The player must not turn the hair away from the string or lift the bow away from the string, but must let the bow *rest* on the string. One must accept the simplicity of the process during which the goal is set, the movement is triggered, and the automatic mechanism is allowed to move the body. During the search for balance, the mental image of the tone should be the guide. It is the quality of this mental image that gives the tone its appropriate sound, because the *image* programs the act of movement.

DÉTACHÉ

It has been said by D. C. Dounis in his book *The Artist's Technique of Violin Playing* that "the détaché is at the same time the simplest and the most important bowing, and the basis for the whole bow technique."[1] Practicing this *legato* stroke gives the player an ideal opportunity to discover the use of the natural balances and to perfect his use of this basic stroke. The détaché is one of the basic gestures of cello playing. This stroke is appropriate to the playing of many musical passages.

When the musical structures require additional articulations,[2] the production of these articulations will emerge from the ability to control the détaché. In every instance, it is the musical design that determines the type of bow stroke to be used.

The gesture which produces the détaché stroke is a movement of the bow arm that divides the bow strokes into various lengths according to the duration of the notes. Indications such as upper half, middle, and lower half are references to areas of action, not literal measurements.

TENDENCY   To consider that all bow movements smaller than the whole bow stroke are produced from segmented parts of the arm.

SOLUTION   To accept all movements of the bow as *parts* of the basic arm stroke on the arc.

---

[1]D.C. Dounis, *The Artist's Technique of Violin Playing* (New York: Carl Fischer, Inc., n.d.), p. 73.

[2]Dr. Dounis' genealogical picture of bow strokes which shows the simple and the accentuated détaché evolving into other articulations can be seen on p. 12 of his book, *The Artist's Technique of Violin Playing.*

SENSATION OF FLOW

One must consider that all bowing movements are derived from the basic stroke in which the arm unfolds (downbow) and folds (upbow). As the player gains an ability to execute each bow movement as a part of the basic movement of folding and unfolding the arm, it will be seen that this act is entirely different from trying to diminish the whole bow stroke and reproducing this miniature with its inherent stroking quality. The cellist must always use the total concept of following the arc while resting the bow on the string, the right arm moving as though it were in "flight," so carefully balanced in its action that it seems to the player to be weightless. From this state, the cellist can eventually use the full potential of automatic bowing.

To proceed with the open-string training of a beginner, one clearly must have musical material—compositional structures that utilize the available musical potential. Upon consideration, the expressive possibility of such structures may be far greater than is first apparent. When playing open-string music, the cellist will encounter an endless variety of musical demands. On any single tone, the player can become aware of the *sensation of flow*. When two notes of the same pitch are connected, the connected quality of movement becomes a musical matter. One must conceptualize this articulation (the attack and release of the notes). When the interval exists between two different strings, the connected quality of movement involves not only the change of bow direction, but the change of arm level as well.

The following interval progression might be used as a basic open-string study. The cellist should vary the tempo and dynamic scheme while investigating a variety of legato and non-legato articulations.

Every aspect of duration can be considered, and all the bow gestures necessary to carrying out these musical ideas can be discovered and practiced. The open-string period of learning can be a dynamic experience both in music-making and cello playing. It is not only the beginner but all cellists interested in the improvement of fundamental skills who should concern themselves with the basic material of open-string playing. Here is an ideal situation for the implementation of New Approach principles regardless of the level of accomplishment of the cellist.

Although teachers have realized the importance of this phase of activity, little pedagogical material is available for our use.[3] One must simply create musical structures to serve the purpose. The music should lend itself to the performance of such things as the basic stroke on one string (downbow and upbow), the connection of two notes on the same string, and the connection of two notes on different strings with both détaché and legato (slurred) bowing.

BOW DISPLACEMENT

The musical fragments should not be played as "bow strokes," but should first be conceptualized as musical sounds of definite musical duration. The displacement of the bow will happen as a result of the musical duration of the note which is both verbally and physically pulsed. The singing of note names acts as a triggering device for the gesture. When the note name is sung, this act will cue the movement of the bow stroke. In this way, the speed of the bow movement will become an integral part of a total gesture that evolves from a musical idea. It is wise to begin with notes of moderate duration. Once the gesture evolves naturally, the musical demands can become varied, and other gestures will develop from those demands. The player should

---

[3]This situation is being corrected by the progressive attitudes of educational endeavors such as the University of Illinois String Research Project. This organization has inspired the creation of such valuable material as *New Tunes for Strings* composed by Fletcher and based on the suggested formulas of Paul Rolland.

proceed from notes of moderate duration to both very long notes and very short notes. The ability to carry out the various musical designs in motion grows with the feelings of confidence engendered by satisfying physical movements which feel good and produce a beautiful tonal result.

Once the basic bow movement has been experienced as a gently undulating opening and closing of the arm (a body movement that is constantly generated by the pulsation of the underlying rhythm), the total configuration of the movement will arouse a sense of physical pleasure. The player will sense the flow of movement from the center of his body to the most distal point of contact where the bow hair touches the vibrating string. This flow of movement is characteristic of the gesture that transforms the musical image into sound. This *feeling of flow* becomes a dominant physical sensation and is completely aligned in time with the temporal aspect of the music.

As the cellist moves from one string to another, the changing arm level evolves naturally. When the player catches the rhythm of the music in his mind, the physical gestures move with that same rhythm, using it as an organizing device. In this way, the bowing gesture becomes rhythmically unified with the musical concept which sets the end-result goal. Since the postural alignment (see page 19) automatically provides for a mobile suspension of the bowing arm, one just "lets it happen" and senses the flow. The player must be vigilant at this point in detecting any conscious and compensating realignments of the shoulders. The cellist must not consciously position the right-arm unit, focusing explicit attention on the particulars of the gesture. If the sitting posture has been arrived at through the search for the fundamental balance of the body over its center of gravity, the gesture will evolve automatically. When this happens spontaneously, the player will only sense the flow of movement, never concerning himself with the conscious directing of positional adjustments. This state of spontaneously-evolving movement with its accompanying sense of flow allows one to dwell exclusively on the musical event, cueing its intervals and pulsing them rhythmically throughout their duration.

VERBAL PULSING

Overt verbal pulsing of the rhythmic duration of notes is essential in the learning period. It gives clarity to the musical image and order to the physical gestures. It assures the proportions of note durations and gives the body a basis for timing its physical movements. One should use monosyllabic sounds to verbalize the rhythmic pulse. The monosyllabic sound has a great deal in common with the musical conception of the beat in regard to duration and quality. The simplicity of the monosyllable makes it a useful ordering device in rhythmic training. Movement gestures can exist in exact temporal concidence with its utterance, or can easily form a temporal counterpoint to it.

The use of the monosyllable (whether overt or covert) in combination with the bowing gestures establishes the musical relationship between the pulse and the gesture. When one allows the movement to evolve on the basis of the pulse of the music, rhythmic expression is assured.

LEFT-HAND ACTION

For the cellist, whether beginner or virtuoso, the performance of a musical interval is the genesis of all technique. With a vivid mental image of the progression of musical intervals, the cellist will set the goals for his body to seek through movement. In the daily practice period, the performer must learn how to handle his desire to move. This daily commitment will be significant when it improves the player's understanding of the music with which he is dealing and enhances his technique—his "feeling" for the instrument.

Kato Havas has adopted the view that the subtlety of one's tone production depends greatly on the ability to conduct the bow strokes from the left hand, where duration and pitch are decided—where the musical ideas are "acted out." If the bowing responds spontaneously to the left-hand action, the musical ideas conceived in one's mind can become physical realities.

HAND POSITION

Acting out the music in the left hand creates the *hand position*. This hand position has a form unique to each individual player depending on his own physical attributes. The form of the hand position must be functional because the left-hand action must successfully change the image of the interval progressions into real sounds. A thorough knowledge of the fingering possibilities is indispensable and will lead to an involuntary physical movement that serves the player's musical intention to great advantage. This knowledge can be gained through a careful study of the intervals that exist in the various positions, and a complete investigation of the methods of combining intervals through in-position playing, extension and shifting.

At the end of the eighteenth century, the cellist John Gunn wrote, "The most varied, complicated, and perfect instrumental performance is resolvable into the accuracy and purity of the several notes that it consists of, and the causes of these qualities into the action of the fingers, in stopping, and of the bow. . ."[4] With this in mind, the first step is to acquaint one's self with the intervals that exist in a certain position and to learn progressively to use their musical potential. From this point, the learning of the entire range of the cello can be done in a logical manner, arrived at through entirely musical means.

---

[4]John Gunn, *The Theory and Practice of Fingering the Violoncello* (London, 1793), p. 59.

THE POSITIONS

There are seven basic placements of the hand in the lower and middle registers on each string. These seven positions have been named by numbers according to the use of the first finger (guide finger) above the open string. As the first four positions of the lower register (the neck positions) are encompassed, one ascends on the string to the place where the neck of the cello joins the body of the instrument. The middle register contains fifth, sixth, and seventh positions. Here it is possible to employ a variety of fingering systems, for unlike the neck positions, a whole tone can be played between the second and third fingers. The higher positions utilize the thumb. This use of the thumb must be cultivated, for it offers numerous fingering possibilities and is the key to complete mastery of the left-hand action. It enables the player to use the entire range of the instrument.

CONTROL CENTER

While examining the left arm, one can move the fingers vigorously, and can observe that movement ripples throughout the entire forearm to the very attachment of the muscles in the elbow region. This rippling may make it seem that the fingers start at the elbow. In searching for an appropriate area for consideration of the left-hand action, Kato Havas realized that we must seriously consider the knuckles. It is from these joints that the brain controls the movements of the fingers.

During performance, the fingers move at the knuckles so that the music is acted out physically. This acting out of the music is the stage of technique when the aural perceptions transformed into physical movement are finally turned into sound. Of course this is not to say that the entire physical aspect of the technique takes place in the knuckles. It *is* to say that one can unify the cello technique by *attending from the knuckles to the fingertips*,[5] where the final expression of the gestures takes

[5] Study Michael Polanyi's discussion of the *semantic aspect* of tacit knowing in his book *The Tacit Dimension*, p. 12.

place. This provides an effective and simple channel of action.

The contact between fingertip and string is the action that completes the left-hand movement in cello technique. This action can be easily observed by the player because it happens in the line of vision. The hand positions that are created by this action with its variable movement are curiously interesting to watch. Not only is the fingertip action beautiful to the eye, but our hearing apparatus causes us to direct our entire body movement to any area from which we imagine sound to emanate. Unfortunately the tendency for the performer to engage his attention in observing this fingertip-string relationship is often encouraged in orthodox training. It is a symptom of conscious cortical direction of the physical act and one that can be withdrawn from the performance experience.

TACTILE RESPONSE

The New Approach involves the player with the act of touching the instrument in such a way that he becomes totally committed to a spontaneous awareness of the points of contact between fingertips and strings. The left-hand gestures (which give physical form to the music) culminate in a tactile experience that sends back information endlessly to the nervous system, which is constantly modulating movement. The body becomes the transmitter of music, and the tactile awareness allows sensory feedback to constantly organize the automatic machinery of the living body. The player soon enjoys "feeling" the music passing through his body in gestures, and he ceases to observe the physical acts visually for the sake of directing them consciously.

It is an illusion that it is possible to direct the action of the fingertip while bypassing the rest of the body. It is impossible to integrate these fragmented or localized physical acts (which are cortically controlled) into the natural cooperation of the limbs. Combined with certain emotional aspects of performance such as the fear of failure, cortical control of these fragmented acts leads to a non-communicative way of playing.

The desire to be secure in the positioning of the fingertips on the fingerboard may cause the player to apply pressure at the point of contact. It is the nature of our tactile response that we react to the hardness of the fingerboard with hardness in the fingertip where there is no movement. Once the fingertip is crushed into the string, there is a tendency to increase the use of the oscillating vibrato movements. This comes about because the pressure of the fingertip stops our natural movement, and we desire to move so greatly that we express this desire with a further insistence on this vibrato movement, regardless of the musical effect. A repetition of this cycle of errors will result in a general stiffness, an unmusical use of the vibrato, and the creation of a tone production which is not satisfactory.

It is in the mind that the musical decisions are made. The physical movements must evolve naturally. Kato Havas' frequently heard admonition "Let it happen!" is the cue. If one lets it happen, that is, allows the movement to evolve naturally, the gesture unfolds as a total cooperation of the limbs with a perfectly integrated positional substrate. We must guarantee an open channel for the transforming of musical concepts into sounds. We must cope effectively with the passing of time, for music is temporal in nature. We in fact program the gestures in a temporal sequence based on the rhythm of the music. When we let it happen subcortically, the culmination of the gestures in the touching of the instrument feeds back sensory information to constantly modulate the movements.

One can readily see that each time a finger is dropped or lifted in cello playing, it is an action in the muscle groups which activate the knuckle and give the total movement pattern positional support that has permitted the finger to move. The finger is only a transmitter of movement that has already been expressed in various locations, but most recently in the knuckle. Musical necessity dictates the physical quality of the gesture. The acting out of the music in gestures has an infinite variety of meanings. When the player removes the potential for pressing downward on the fingertips by dropping the knuckles below the fingertips and "hanging" the fingers onto the fingerboard, it is possible to control the weight of the finger on the string from an area removed from the point of contact. This removes any desire for excessive weight on the string after the fingertip has arrived in contact. Localized pressing of this type interferes with minute adjustments necessary to expressive intonation. It stiffens the hand and blocks the transmission of energy which should flow easily through the limbs.

It is not a question of strength that determines a successful technique, yet generations of players have followed the credo "I must practice to make my fingers strong!" The balanced hand and the resilient, sensitive touch release one from the idea that the fingertip-string relationship is immediately responsible for musical results. The fingertips become integrated into the total physical gesture, and their touching is both the final expression of a movement, and the means by which sensory feedback is sent to the nervous system, which modulates movement.

INTONATION

Playing out of tune is such a common phenomenon that musicians tend to speak of intonation only in terms of "bad intonation." The intoning of the music is the primary objective of the player. That music is "in tune" or "out of tune" is quite an easy assessment to make, but to say why it is in or out of tune is another matter. To give the impression of playing in tune, the pitch of each note must be meaningfully related to that of another. It is our inner musical voice that perceives the relationships in the interval progressions. When the fingers have been directed to the fingerboard through the action of the automatic mechanism, it becomes a matter for the mind's comparator (match/mismatch) to reveal the success of the gesture in carrying out the goal of the musical ideation.

The fingertip must not be committed to an unmovable point of contact. There can really be no more than an approximation of the location of the point of contact on the fingerboard. The player must "search" for the note's quality. The contact between fingertip and string must be pliant. The inner musical voice programs the act of the body, and the spontaneous gestures transform the musical concepts into sounds. The final expression of these gestures is the pliant touch of the fingertip. One can begin to enjoy the physical pleasure of a plastic connection at the point of contact once the knuckle-fingertip relationship is established. This relationship gives the player a sense of "hanging" the fingertips on the fingerboard, holding them in place by a weight from below.[6]

ASPECTS OF TONE

If we are to attribute to physical movement the ability to express our impressions of tone, then the various components of the tone must be controlled from a central point. Consideration of every aspect of the tone production must be conveyed in the total physical gesture. If the case is otherwise, the unification of the technique can never be complete. The movement of the knuckle is a part of a total response. It is in the positioning of the knuckle that one finds the freedom to convey his concepts through gesture. One of the major aspects of the New Approach is that parts of the total response are not isolated for focal attention during performance. When one creates the postural attitude which lends itself to movement, and allows the gestures to evolve naturally, the body is allowed to spontaneously express the mind's concepts.

What are the various aspects of tone which must be conceptualized? The pitch, dynamic, duration and the tone quality arising from the combination of these elements give the tone its character. These aspects of the note's character form its *identity*. We must identify each note before it is played.

The *pitch* of a given note is first revealed by the inner musical

---

[6]When one uses the *thumb positions* it is no longer possible to drop the knuckles lower than the fingertips and a different relationship is established which removes the leverage that invites a direct downward pressure on the fingerboard. One hoists the knuckle above and behind the fingertip, leaning the knuckle slightly toward the scroll.

voice. It is not revealed as an abstraction. We imagine the inner voice to sing this pitch. The goal for finding the pitch is then set. Our body must make a gesture which will allow the knuckle to drop a finger onto the approximate point on the string which will produce the desired pitch. From that point it is a matter of feeling with the fingertip. A plastic connection between fingertip and string allows for the full potential of the search to be carried out. What is learned in the form of sensory information is automatically fed back to the mechanism of the body which monitors our physical gestures.

The *dynamic* of the given note is revealed by the same method. One imagines the volume of the tone, and this sets the goal once more for the physical expression. Once the knuckles are favorably positioned, the muscles drop the finger into place, activating a programmed movement. This movement is programmed with an appropriate thrust known to produce the desired dynamic through the coordinated action of the bow. The weight of the finger is established instantaneously in this subcortical calculation, and the bow responds with a movement that has coordinated equivalent properties.

The *duration* of the note is accomplished as it is conceived in our image with the insistence of the regular beat or pulsation which takes place in the mind and is reinforced by the physical gesture. The pulsing of the note will occur physically wherever there is a movement outlet for it. On the left side, it may express itself most obviously in the vibrato movements, and on the right side it may occur in a subtle undulation of the upper arm which is perfectly related to the total arm movement. Again, the vibrato movements and the undulating arm movements are parts, easily observed, of a total body movement which is regulating the balance spontaneously.

The *tone quality* of the note is decided by the total synthetic effect of the other elements, pitch, dynamic and duration. This complex of elements with its varying intensity and fluctuations influences our whole mental attitude when we are assessing the tone quality.

Perhaps there will never be a satisfactory physical definition of what is a "good tone." The tone quality of a given note is a condition already influenced by certain unification of the technique before the actual sound is heard by the player. However, we do know that it is the performer's appraisal of that tone quality that gives him a greater understanding of his effort. We also know that appraisal is made by hearing a tone quality emerge that is an artistic representation of the mental image held in the mind. This successful approximation propels one toward a new dimension in performing. Producing a beautiful tone has a self-generating effect on our spirit.

3 Finger Preparation

THE LEFT THUMB

The use of the left thumb as a mobile point of balance and the positioning of the knuckles are major aspects of the left-hand technique. If there is a direct vertical pressure imposed on the string by the fingertip, there will be a corresponding upward pressure from the left thumb, for this is the pinching action of the hand. With each note that is played with such pressure and counterpressure, tension accumulates, and although it is sometimes possible to force one's self to manipulate the instrument in this way while staying in a given position, when it becomes necessary to shift to another position, or to use an extension, the cellist will be at a great physical disadvantage.

The cellist should relate the thumb of the left hand to the fingers in the same way that he did in finding the bow hold with the right hand. It will only be necessary to keep the thumb loosely related to the neck of the cello, using it to create a sensitive balance with the four fingers working from their knuckles. When the thumb and the fingers find their appropriate relation to each other through balance, the thumb becomes a valuable ally in the search for tone production. If it clamps and presses upward, it becomes an uncontrollable obstacle to playing.

Experimentation without the cello will show that the motion of the fingers falling on the thumb creates the opening and closing of a round hole.[1] Nature has provided a considerable distance between the thumb and the index finger. The resilience of the fingers opening and closing against the thumb has a springing action that is essential to the left-hand technique.

---

[1]Kato Havas, *The Twelve Lesson Course* (London: Bosworth and Co. Ltd., 1964), p. 27.

TENDENCY   To collapse the "hole" when pressure is increased
           in the fingertip or thumb. The thumb draws up tightly
           against the fingerboard and the knuckles push inward
           toward the neck, rendering the joints immobile.

SOLUTION   To constantly "open the circle." This allows the
           muscles attached to the thumb and fingers to relax, and
           frees the action of all the joints.

As the playing skill is increased and elaborated, it becomes
important that this basic configuration is used. When ascending
past the fourth position through the seventh position, the thumb
must sometimes leave its place behind the neck of the cello. It
then moves with the hand as it passes over the body of the cello.
In the thumb positions, the neck of the cello no longer separates
the thumb and fingers, and this circular opening helps relate the
thumb to the fingers and gives a natural elevation to the four
knuckles and fingers. It is known that when the thumb and side
of the hand clamp together, the tension moves upward along the
kinematic chain and freezes the wrist, the elbow, and the
shoulder.

BASIC SHAPES OF THE HAND POSITION

As one alternately plays the semitone and the whole tone
with the first and second fingers, the hand will begin to assume
its basic shapes. The spacing between the first and the second
fingers will depend entirely on the size of the musical interval
being played. With this in mind, one recognizes that playing a
semitone between the first and second finger shapes the hand into
what has been called the *closed hand position,* while playing a
whole tone between these fingers shapes the hand into the *open
hand position.* It is in the acting out of the musical intervals that
form follows function, and the gestures of the left hand give
reason for the two basic shapes of the hand position. These two
basic shapes are never static because in each position on the
string the player is dealing with a different string length and

consequently a different relative spacing of the fingers. The primary consideration in adopting these two basic hand shapes with their different spacings between the first and second fingers is that the spacing between any other two fingers (between second and third, third and fourth) is reserved for playing *semitones only* in the lower positions.

SEMITONES

Semitones can be played by any combination of consecutive fingers. Using the first and second fingers, the player can perform not only semitones, but whole tones as well. The proper spacing of the fingers comes naturally from learning to play various combinations of semitones and whole tones, and in doing this the cellist can learn the basic procedures of *finger preparation.* Skill in the use of the finger preparation must be applied to every aspect of the left-hand technique, for it is the foundation of cello playing. It is in the preparation of each finger that one moves through the interval progressions, acting out the music in the left-hand gestures. In this skill of finger preparation, each finger acts as a key to unlock the action of the next finger to be used.

TENDENCY   To apply a downward pressure on the fingertip, spreading the fingers apart and holding the hand in a set position.

SOLUTION   To position the knuckles so that the fingers curl, and so that the fingertips are held in place by a feeling of weight in the knuckles below. Each finger is thrust forward toward the bridge with a ballistic movement; the feeling of weight in the knuckle determines the contact between fingertip and string.

"The further away the source of this weight is placed, the more the fingertip is released from its immediate responsibility and the easier it is to find the quality of tone the music happens to demand . . . the actual contact between the fingertip and string is so delicate that the free and regular vibration of the fundamental note and its 'harmonics' is assured and there is a definite sound of vibrato, with no undue and conscious oscillation of the wrist, hand or arm. It is a very good practice first to sing the intervals, then to learn to *hear* them, without making any sound at all. For if the mind is developed to anticipate the right pitch and quality of sound, the fingers will follow the demand of the mind."[1]

If the postural substrate has been cultivated and the consequence includes the arms in a state of mobile suspension, power will flow from the torso throughout the body network *through* the finger into the instrument. The physical gesture which is identifiable with each musical interval played will have *movement* as its primary characteristic. During the learning period, the player programs these gestures, so that conscious directing of the music will cue them into reality.

One should begin by playing an ascending semitone progression between the first and second finger, playing the lower note of the interval with the first finger. If there is no obstacle holding the flow of energy in check, the tone should pour from the instrument and should be resonant and responsive to the player's imagination. During the life of this tone, all thoughts are excluded from the conscious mind except one. This thought propels the tone through time.

"NAMING THE NOTE"

Singing the note's name (with the inner musical voice) cues the beginning of the gesture, and *pulsing the note* rhythmically keeps the gesture operative throughout the duration of the tone. The displacement of the bow is coordinated with the pulsing left-hand gesture; the entire body is alive with motion as the player "feels" the gesture transforming his idea into sound. This sensory perception feeds back information which does not intrude into the consciousness, but does keep the mechanism of

---

[1]Havas, *A New Approach to Violin Playing,* p. 31.

the living body modulated and operative. To cue the next step in the playing of the interval progression, *sing the new note name.* Inward singing of the note names is not just a matter of identification of the notes. Identifying of the note is done in a number of ways (including the obvious one of taking a visual cue from "reading the music"). Singing the note names is not a vague or passive action. It not only serves as a cue for the triggering of the gesture, but pulsing of the note fills out the time which must elapse to ascertain the musical duration of the tone.

To give a simple example: if one intends to play an "E" with the duration of four beats (whole note) in a moderate tempo, then the inner musical voice sings, "E-bahm-bahm-bahm." The singing of the note's name ("E") cues the beginning of the physical gesture; the consequent monosyllabic singing of the pulsing syllable propels it through time. When one has allowed the inner musical voice to occupy itself in this way, one has excluded everything from the consciousness except the musical thought which is totally pertinent to the task at hand.

In order to cue the second stage of the interval, one simply sings the name of the new note (in this case "F") and then the pulsing syllables. Allow the body to respond to this mental direction. Since one has programmed the appropriate gesture to act out this bit of music, just LET IT HAPPEN.

"PULSING THE NOTE"

There is always the question of just how the implementation of New Approach cue devices "works." First it should be clearly understood that at the outset, this device of singing the note's name should be overt. One should sing *aloud* the entire device AWAY FROM THE CELLO. Then one should repeat the process PLAYING THE CELLO. The overt activity reinforces what might otherwise be vague or unformed. Finally, the device becomes totally contained—interiorized—but retains its original dynamic quality. There is every indication that until this device is habituated, there is danger of its use fading in favor of concentration on the particulars of the physical action. Players who have not reached the point of habitual use (and one must always remember that the New Approach is a training) are often concerned with the control of the device when playing rapid notes. To the player who has little or no experience with the device, even in the playing of slowly-moving intervals where there is no sense of hurry, the idea of naming the notes with rapidity is a bit worrying. Suffice it to say that the habituating of the device is progressive. First one learns to deal with it in notes of long duration and in an overt fashion, singing and pulsing the sounds with the real singing voice. As confidence and skill are gained through actually vocalizing the musical materials, the ability to carry it out rapidly and covertly follows.

This ordering device has both a purpose in the triggering of the physical gestures, and in the clarification of the musical concept. To speak further of the gesture which acts out the semitone, the action of the second finger will cause a change of balance in the hand. The first finger, having done its part in the performance of the interval, is released from its holding activity. The concentration of the mind and the activity of the body is exactly aligned with the musical happening of the moment. When the first finger is not actually playing a note, it rests lightly in position, unlocked and ready for further use as the music demands.

TENDENCY   To press the finger into the string to assure the hand position. This eventually leads to undue tension in that finger. Should the player return to it, he will simply "fall into a dead note," for the finger will be pinned down and unable to respond to his musical demand.

SOLUTION   To concentrate the mental activity and the physical gesture on *only* the musical note and finger that is currently in use. One keeps the unused finger free from immobility by release. (In fast passages, the unused finger will remain in contact with the string, but this contact must be light and pliant, and the finger must be allowed to pulse on demand.)

When the second finger takes over the action of the music, the first finger will "unfurl," the balance of weight changing from one finger to the other. Because the contact between fingertip and string is pliant and free of pressure, the player can search for the note—search for its every musical characteristic. This is an intrinsic part of the mobile gesture. This mobility goes on during the entire duration of the note and gives vitality to the tone production. The searching for expressive intonation, physical comfort, and a sensitive vibrato (one that is given mobility through the rhythmic pulsation) is characteristic of the New Approach procedures.

WHOLE TONES

To play a whole-tone interval with these same fingers, a different preparation is necessary. The second finger will be dropped into place with a different thrust. The difference is in the configuration of the new pattern, and the subcortical centers must program what is needed.

TENDENCY   To stretch the fingers when the points of contact are widely separated. Spreading the fingers apart and pressing downward increases the tension between the fingers.

SOLUTION   To position the knuckles so that the hand "opens" below the fingertip, not above it.

When the knuckles are dropped lower than the fingertips, and the new finger is thrown forward, "hooking" the fingertips into the strings with a light and sensitive touch, the gesture creates a feeling of thrust, holding the fingertip in place with a plastic connection at the point of contact. If the positioning is appropriate to this new configuration, the movements will evolve naturally, and will approximate the image of the interval. The point of contact between the fingertip and the string is greatly influenced by the player's ability to allow the body to retain its natural curving forms. As the joint is made mobile, the finger

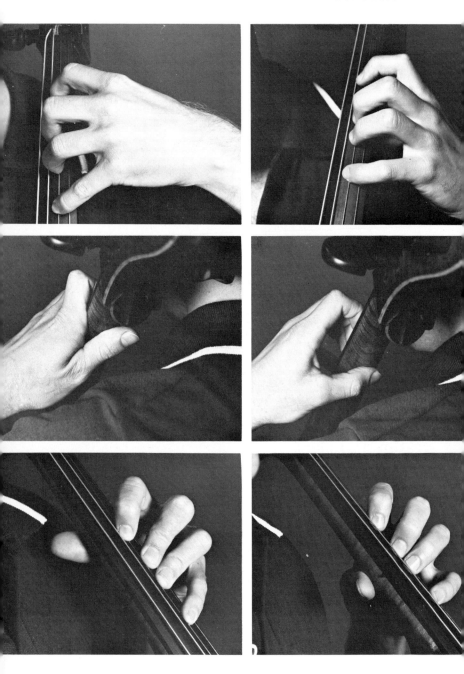

curls. The final contact with the string occurs nearer the joining of the closely-cut fingernail and the fleshy endpad as the finger assumes its natural arching. Very often players who suffer from "double joints" or weak joints can assist themselves by allowing no angularity in the finger. As the curled finger hooks into the string, the weight of the hand drops below (does not press down on the finger), and one can swing on the finger, still keeping the natural arching. Even the slightest rigidity in the final joint of the finger will place an obstacle in the way of the flow of energy and will cause immobility and its consequent tension.

The mind is always occupied with a sequence of interval progressions of varying sizes. It perceives the progression of sounds in the order of their happening. The New Approach is primarily concerned with order. Knowing the possibilities of finger placement on the fingerboard is absolutely indispensable. Unless one learns to use these possibilities to a musical advantage, there can be no real artistic achievement. During performance, the mind must be totally occupied with musical images, and the technique must be held only in the service of those musical ideas.

Confusion, fatigue and anxiety can arise from the complications of dropping and lifting fingers, moving them from side to side in string crossings, stretching and pressing them, and pinning them into synthetic forms. The New Approach places the concentration on the musical happening of the moment as the balance shifts from one finger to another. The progression of the musical ideas (sound to sound) and the progression of the physical gestures (touch to touch) must be coordinated into a unified cycle of events. One does not perform physically what has already happened, or what is about to happen, but only *what is happening*. In this way, music is unfolded in time. The finger that has *already* played is released, unlocked for future action. Every new finger is prepared in the action of the new gesture always in cycle with the rhythm of the music. Each note in the interval progressions has a life of its own and is logically related to the temporal nature of music through rhythm. Through this freedom of movement comes the ability to use the body's real power to express one's musical concepts. When the player understands how to cope with his desire to implement his musical ideas, he will allow his power to pulse throughout a network of muscles and joints that does not resist movement.

What must be clear is that the key to understanding and using a controlled finger action is the acceptance of the dual nature of *each* movement that produces a musical interval on the cello.

THRUST AND RELEASE

Thrust depends on the size of the interval and therefore on the consequent distance between its two pitches. Whether the interval is large or small, the finger preparation will carry the new finger to the new note with a forward action toward the bridge. It will be seen that string crossing and shifting are simply variations of this basic finger preparation skill.

Release is equally important. It is sometimes relegated to a secondary position or even overlooked entirely, although it is an integral aspect of the finger action. To explain the release on a musical basis, one need only realize that the musical note being played must be related to the finger that is carrying out the gesture. When one pins down a note that is no longer functioning musically, one moves away from a musically-oriented technique. Pressing a musically inactive finger into the fingerboard in order to hold a synthetic hand position intact defeats the ability to create a changing balance between various fingers. When the note is finished, the release of the finger must be related to the finger that is carrying out the next action. One creates true independence of the fingers by properly relating their action to the music-making.

One cannot profitably describe this dual action without stressing that the gesture which acts it out is triggered by one cue only—the singing of the note name by the inner musical voice. As the gesture is acted out, the critical point in musical time is reached to move on to a new pitch (known through the pulsing of the note being played). The next gesture is cued by singing

the name of the *next* note in the interval chain. The cue triggers
the thrust. The musical termination of the pitch triggers the
release. In this sense there is thrust and release for each pitch
performed. These gestures shape each note, giving it an articu-
lated beginning and ending. The thrust-release gesture is the
basic unit used in this architectural interpretation of music. Its
physical action defines each musical interval in a chain of intervals that creates the larger forms of music.

The physical action is put out of cycle with the musical
event when the new note of an interval receives no impulse. The
bow cannot respond automatically to a left-hand pitch that has
no impulse. The pinning down of inactive fingers in the left-hand
gesture (instead of giving them vitality and movement) causes
the player to push and pull the bow consciously to activate the
music. The explicit focal attention of the mind must be on the
directing of the music, not on the manipulation of the bow stroke.
From the outset, the cellist must deal with the thrust and release
of *every note*. The physical gestures are as varied as the intervals
themselves, but the control is constant. When one accepts the
simplicity of the idea, it becomes a dynamic occupation to deal
with each note on this basis, building up the progression of
intervals into larger musical forms. One programs each gesture,
directs the musical event, and "lets it happen" physically.

The physical quality of the thrust and release gestures varies
according to the nature of the music being played. When there is
no time to actually disengage the fingertip from the string, the
feeling of thrust and release is utilized. The contact between
fingertip and string must be so pliant that the finger can pulse
on demand while keeping its contact with the string, even if the
tip of the finger is not physically released from the string. If it
is otherwise, the cellist will find himself often falling onto dead
notes in the interval chain. When the new note in the sequence
cannot be pulsed by the thrust (or the feeling of thrust) because
it is crushed into the string, the coordination between the finger
and bow is destroyed. If this happens one will often move the
bow inappropriately to compensate for the disturbed coordination.
This all leads the player to draw his attention away from the

musical direction of the performance and to focus his awareness on the particulars of the physical gesture.

One benefit of this type of action is clarity in rapid passages, because the gestures are programmed in such a way as to insure a unified method of tone production. All intervals are produced with the same physical method, and each has its appropriate vitality. The player puts his musical concepts and his physical gestures into the same time cycle, and both the mind and the body are therefore put entirely in the service of the temporal aspect of the music.

By dealing always with the interval unit, the player will allow no segmented part of the musical architecture to go unnoticed. The physical gestures are constantly negotiating the movement of the basic components of the musical structure. The finger action will be exactly related to the musical image held in the mind. When the mind and the body are coordinated to work in this way, the musical ideas will emerge in a positive physical form. Once fundamental skills have been mastered, there is no need for cortical control of the physical aspects of playing. The mind will issue the orders which automatically program the acts needed. These acts evolve naturally because the physical gestures allow the player the sensuous pleasure of touching the instrument, "knowing" the feel of the technical procedures through the gestures rather than thinking about them and directing them from the mind.

The most "advanced" aspects of the physical movement are simply variations of the application of these basic skills. For instance, it will be seen that the act of finger preparation with its duality of thrust and release can be transformed and expanded in endless variation to include shifting, string crossing and all the details of technique so often considered as segmented particulars in the orthodox training of cellists.

DESCENDING INTERVALS

The posture described earlier allows for an automatic mobile suspension of the arms, positioning the knuckles in relation to the fingertips in such a way that the plane of activity of the finger action can be conceptualized as moving from "behind the scroll toward the bridge." This is quite a different matter from a positioning which puts the knuckles above the fingertips.

When playing descending semitones and whole tones, special consideration must be given to the forward action of the fingers as they are thrust toward the bridge. As one descends, the higher-numbered finger must be released, and the lower-numbered finger (which completes the interval progression) must be given a *definite thrust*. With this impulse, the physical gesture can be aligned with the musical movement expressed in the interval progression. If the playing of descending intervals in-position is thoughtfully organized, the player will be greatly assisted in the more elaborate skill of *shifting* in descending intervals. From the playing of semitones and whole tones, both ascending and descending, the cellist can learn the entire gamut of left-hand technique. Gestures are programmed for shifting, string crossing, double stopping, glissando, and so on. The natural evolution through gestures of these left-hand skills (identifiable with musical architecture) will happen spontaneously in the course of performing.

4 Reflex Bowing

COORDINATION OF THE HANDS

The reflex movement of the bow is coordinated with the action of the left-hand gesture that transforms all the tonal-rhythmic aspects of the interval progressions. These left-hand gestures explicitly determine the duration of the note, and the bow sustains that duration because the two separate acts are coordinated. In this sense, one "conducts" the bow from the left hand.

TENDENCY   To combine involuntary reflexive bow movements with consciously directed bow movements, alternating the attention between the left hand and the bow.

SOLUTION   To give impulse to every note performed in the interval sequence through the left-hand gesture, and to allow the bow movement to react as a reflex to these impulses.

When only some of the notes are receiving an impulse in the left hand, the remainder of the notes demand no response from the bow. When no response is demanded, it is of course necessary to consciously motivate the bow. This mixture of procedures causes the tone production to be varied in quality. The acts of both sides of the body must be integrated spontaneously by the nervous system, and the living machinery must be allowed to carry out its operations without conscious direction.

Like the various "advanced" left-hand skills, the numerous articulations of the bow can emerge naturally from increased musical demands. Spiccato strokes, both the thrown and the springing types, depend on the vitality of the impulse in the left-hand gesture to a greater degree than is usually acknowledged by players. When the player controls the physical act, cortically concentrating on a series of quick movements in both the left-hand gesture and the bow action, the explicit focal attention is diverted from the identification of the notes as they exist in the musical image. The mind must dwell on the musical matters, not the mechanical ones.

BOW RHYTHM

It is worthwhile to note that due to the sustaining action of bowing (whether the notes being performed are short or long), there is an intimate physical relationship with the tone production *throughout the duration of each note*. The bowing is in some ways akin to the breathing of singers or wind-instrument players. The striking thing is that no more than a mechanical rhythm can be produced with the bowing if the bow movement is not an integral part of the total bodily response. Since the bow has no ability to create intervals (other than those formed by the use of the open strings), it does not have the same vital importance as the left hand in establishing the subtlety of duration resulting from the expressive aspect of the interval progression. Musical rhythm exists when one sings a progression of intervals. Because the intervals are of varying sizes, i.e., the distance between their tonal points of reference varies, one feels that each interval takes its own musical time to exist. The left hand can learn to sense this phenomenon if its gesture is transforming a musical image which is sung by the inner musical voice. Since the bow has no ability to create intervals, it must carry out its characteristic task —that of sustaining sounds—on the basis of duration decided by the left-hand action.

The problems arising from this situation can be exemplified. When rhythmic command is given directly to the bowing action in a rapid spiccato passage, the performer often "chases after speed." If the bow alternates strokes with a mechanical precision, the bow rhythm will seldom coincide with the expressive rhythm of the interval progression. When the controlling rhythmic factor is the reiterated bow stroke rather than the multiconfigured left-

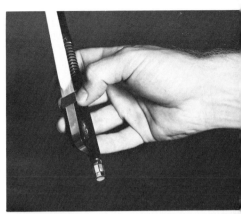

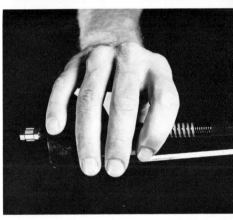

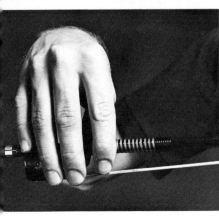

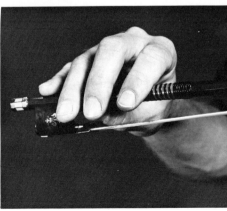

hand gesture, the passage will probably sound unmusical. In this case, the most obvious rhythm will be that of the bow change rather than that of the rhythmic structure of the interval progression. In the case of string crossing, the bow must have a common programming with the left-hand gesture, because while the distance between the strings and the action of the crossing bow remain constant, the intervals vary in their shapes and are created with impulses that are expressive rather than mechanical.

When the body understands through experience the different aspects carried out by the two sides, then one wants these different aspects of the one total act integrated centrally before the specific right and left orders flow to the parts implicated in the act. When the left-hand gestures become convincing transformations of the interval progressions being sung by the inner musical voice, all is well. If the bowing is characterized by movement which is free from undue stress and localized pressure, the effectiveness of this integration will be heard in a tone production which is a musically convincing approximation of the mental image.

The mental-physical abandon brought about by the use of spontaneous bowing offers quick and lasting results both to the beginner and to the advanced player dealing with complex articulations. The tone production resulting from the integration of the actions of both sides is quite different from that which results from a mechanical motivation in the bowing arm itself, which is cortically controlled and does not evolve naturally.

Some players experience anxiety over the fact that their tone becomes "wooden" when executing complex articulations that are controlled cortically with full focal attention. One frequently hears spiccato passages that are brittle and lack resonance and vitality. If one brings conscious effort to the maneuvering of the bow during complex articulations, he may segment the movements of the arm, causing himself to move the bow ahead or behind the rhythmic action of the left-hand gestures. When spontaneous, reflexive bowing is used, the quality of tone produced in spiccato and springing staccato passages is as lustrous and vibrant as that produced in the more elementary articulations.

5 *Interval Progressions*

FINGERING

When he uses all the fingers, the player becomes aware that there is a disparity in their relative size and strength. However, the cello technique does not demand the same activity from all the fingers. Jean Louis Duport codified the modern system of fingering as early as 1819 in his monumental work, *Essai sur le Doigté du Violoncelle.*[1] At this time a method of fingering evolved that used the fingers according to natural potential. For instance, one uses the strong first finger in a much different role than the relatively weaker and smaller fourth finger. It should not be the intention of the player to exercise the fingers in such a way that they can be made equal. On the contrary, the player must discover his own hand through touching the cello. Once he begins to have a strong impression of his own unique hand, then he must learn to balance and position it in such a way that his left-hand gestures make full use of his own potential for movement.

In this century Diran Alexanian in his book *Traité théorique et pratique du Violoncelle*[2] has offered us a treatise which is a veritable *dictionary* of the cello technique. This work, based on the principles accepted by Pablo Casals, draws one's attention to the carefully organized system of *extension* fingerings introduced logically into modern pedagogy by Casals and his pupils. In speaking of the extension fingerings Maestro Casals has related that he once had the opportunity of hearing the cellist Toliansky in Hungary.[3] To Casals' surprise this gypsy musician was using

---

[1]Jean Louis Duport, *Essai sur le Doigté du Violoncelle* (Paris: A. Cotelle, 1819).

[2]Diran Alexanian, *Traité théorique et pratique du Violoncelle* (Paris: Editions Salabert, 1922).

[3]J. Ma. Corredor, *Conversations with Casals* (New York: E. P. Dutton and Co., Inc., 1956), p. 60.

all the fingering by extension. Toliansky had come to this by pure intuition and was no doubt influenced by the size of his own hand and his unique musical inclinations. This innovation of the extension fingering was arrived at by Casals and Toliansky to meet the same end result: greater flexibility in connecting widely-spaced tones existing in the interval progressions.

Because of the size of the cello, the fingering possibilities in the neck positions are quite different from those of the smaller violin and viola. In the first position, one normally plays no interval larger than the major third between the first and fourth finger on the same string. The first and fourth finger form the outlines of a position, while the second and third fingers each serve on alternate occasions to perform the semitones enclosed in the interval of the third (played by the first and fourth finger).

Except in chromatic progressions when the four fingers are used consecutively, the player must always make a choice between the second and third finger when bridging this melodic interval of the third. It is upon this principle that the fingering system is built. The cellist should never grope on the fingerboard. An inner knowledge of these patterns is important, and will grow organically from the actual playing of various intervals.

When the interval of the third is major rather than minor, the first and fourth fingers are separated by a greater distance. The player relies on the natural size and strength of the first finger in spanning the larger interval. In this case, the second finger is given a different finger preparation, and sent a whole tone away from the first finger to bridge the diatonic gap between the outlying notes of the major third.

THE SCALES

The playing of scales is an ideal way to perform consecutive movement of small intervals, and in doing so, to habituate the use of the various configurations which define the closed or open hand position. If the preparatory study is done with attention to tone production, the player can learn to use the scales in an infinite variety of ways. One should never allow scale playing to become a mechanized exercise. As long as the player is deeply involved in the continuous recreation of musical ideas through a concentrated effort to realize the full potential of all interval progressions, the scales will be a valuable source of study material.

RELEASE OF FOURTH FINGER

When the interval progression demands movement from the fourth finger to an adjacent open string, careful attention must be given to the release of the fourth finger from the string. It is necessary to exaggerate this release action before moving to the open-string note. Since no finger is used to play the open string, the release of the previously-used finger will form the gesture that creates the interval between the fourth finger and the open string. If the fourth finger is pinned down, there will be no left-hand gesture—only stillness. This state leaves nothing to coordinate the bow movement and the left-hand action; the bow movement will become dominant, and the rhythm of the bow movement may easily overcome the rhythm of the interval progression. The pinned-down, immobile fourth finger disturbs the normal event of coordinated left-hand gesture and bow movement.

Before playing the scales, the basic principles of finger preparation must be habituated. Since the span of the scales requires crossing from one string to another, the player must let the bow arm find the proper arm level for each string. With the bow arm, it is the placement of the upper arm that "finds" the level for each string. The right arm must be constantly searching for balance and feeling the sensation of flow as the bow crosses to a new string.

ARPEGGIOS

To practice interval progressions containing minor and major thirds and perfect fourths, the cellist should play arpeggios built on the minor and major triads formed on the tonic note of the scales. Later a further study can be made of the arpeggios by playing those built on the dominant and the diminished-seventh chords.

STRING CROSSING

When an interval is played utilizing two different strings, both the fingers and the bow must move from one string to another. The technique of *string crossing* promotes an apparent "side to side" visual movement of the fingers and a change of arm level for the bowing which often gives rise to problems. It is important to realize that the fingers working from their knuckles don't go "side to side" but sustain their movement in a plane from scroll to bridge. If during string crossing the bow keeps its contact with the string through proper use of the natural balances, it will never arrive too late or too early to play the second note of the interval progression. Both sides are programmed simultaneously to create the interval progression. This is integrated automatically when the body is in a state of natural balance. The coordination happens spontaneously because both sides are creating the rhythm of the interval gestured in the left hand.

One effective practice procedure is to prepare the new finger and send it forward to a note on the same string. This first step assures the proper thrust forward toward the bridge. When the forward movement can be done with conviction, the player gives a greater thrust and sends the finger *forward* (not across) to its *real target,* completing the interval progression.

This technique is particularly useful in the preparation of descending intervals that occur simultaneously with the descending shifts.

Crossing from a given string to a *lower* string takes a different preparation than crossing to a *higher* string due to the conformation of the hand and its placement to the left of the fingerboard. For instance, when one crosses to a higher string (with a higher numbered finger) to complete an interval progression, the finger that plays the final note of the progression will be nearer its target because the knuckles are positioned to the left of the fingerboard near the highest string. On the other hand, when a higher-numbered finger must cross to a *lower* string to complete an interval progression, it must travel farther to reach its target and therefore, it must receive a larger preparation. However, both crossings are accomplished with the same basic finger movement. ONLY THE SIZE OF THE PREPARATION VARIES. The cellist must remember that no progression of musical intervals should result from a mechanical movement. The inner musical voice must identify each interval with conviction, and this will serve as the command which sets the body in motion.

HALF POSITION

When the cellist is completely familiar with the possibilities of finger preparation in the first position, and can apply his knowledge to the expressive playing of interval progressions in that position, it is a comparatively simple task to adapt this knowledge to the use of the half position, which lies *between* the first position and the open strings. The first finger (guide finger) plays the pitches which are a semitone above the open string, and the internal relationship of the fingering possibilities remains the same as in the first position. The first and fourth fingers will still encompass minor and major thirds, but the range of pitch of half position is one semitone lower than first position.

The working knowledge of half position is an extremely useful one when playing music written in keys that are not closely related to the keys of less than four sharps or four flats. There are numerous passages that can be played effectively by combining half position and first position. Even without recourse to either extension of the left hand or to the shifting of position, the cellist can perform a great variety of music.

PULSING THE RHYTHM

The constant use of the rhythmic resource assists the performer in organizing his body movements into meaningful gestures. The pulsing of the rhythm with the body must be encouraged because it is an important unifying device in transforming musical concepts into appropriate physical gestures. The pulse that runs through all music must become a physical reality. As these impulses are manifested in physical movement, they affect the entire body. On the left side they surge throughout the entire network of the left arm unit, and are shown in their final form in the fingertip pulsing on the string. It is to this rhythmic pulse that one attaches the subtle change in tone color which we call the *vibrato*. The rhythmic pulsing of the body allows us to generate movement on which the final tone production depends.

VIBRATO

Pedagogues have disagreed both on how to teach the vibrato and on whether or not mechanical exercises designed to initiate the vibrato movements will really lead to the final control of its use. It has been often suggested that the cellist with *no* vibrato can be taught to vibrate by simply listening to the sound of a player's tone which does have vibrato. This implies that the student must listen, then "let it happen," and in this way the vibrato will establish itself through the light sensitive touch of the mobile fingertip. Because each aspect of playing is interlocked with some other, the vibrato will only emerge as an integral part of the tone production if the way has been prepared both in matters of ideation and physical ease of movement.

From the beginning of training, the cellist must conceive a tone production that has the potential for constant and infinite variety. If the body is mobile, if the gesture is meaningful, and if the touch of the fingertip is able to transmit rather than "stop the string," the tones which sound through a definite musical time duration will have the basis for the vibrato from the outset. As the musical insight changes with experience, the body is then ready to spontaneously react to the most subtle ideation. Because there is built into the living machine a comparator, the mismatch between the musical idea and the end-result will always be detected. If the pupil *accepts* a wooden tone, or a monotonous oscillating vibrato, it points to defective perceptual training. If he learns physical movement that will transform his concept of an expressive tone enhanced with vibrato, then he simply must become deeply involved in his self-learning and explore the possibilities of the natural positional substrate that will allow the appropriate gesture to evolve.

Very often as the student *sees the movement effect* of the vibrato, he is tempted to shake the hand, or the wrist, or the arm (or some combination of parts of the left arm unit). If the fingertips are pressing into the string, responding to the hardness of the fingerboard with hardness and tension in the finger itself then the "shaking vibrato" becomes a habit arising from the desire to escape tension through movement. Unfortunately this creates a cycle of tension, and the more one shakes, the more one must press the finger to "hold the pitch" or "keep the hand position." When the pressing increases, the mechanical oscillation must be made with more vigor to break through the resulting immobility. With the use of this type of vibrato, the player becomes conditioned to hearing the monotonous regularity of the sound, and he may soon accept it as inevitable, although it does not reveal the truth of the musical image.

SELF-GENERATING MOVEMENT

The movements which aid the vibrato must be self-generating. Once the *entire* left arm unit is set in motion searching for balance with no immobility in the shoulder, elbow or wrist, such movement is available. Kato Havas has written, "When the vibrato is spontaneous and subject to one's most subtle intentions in creating nuance, the total body movement becomes responsible, and the vibrato is essentially the result of using the balances to a musical advantage . . . I do not claim that there is no movement of vibrato at all, but this free play-action of the base joints (knuckles) assures a flexible and impulsive vibrato which is never learnt separately and which is entirely in the service of the player's musical demands and imagination, regardless of whether he plays cantilena or bravura passages."[4]

It is the rhythmic pulse of the music being played that integrates the vibrato into the total configuration of the left-hand gesture. If the vibrato has an isolated rhythm of its own which is directed cortically, it can never have the *impulsive and flexible quality* that the music demands. As the beat of the music is pulsed through the gesture, this pulsation finds its final expression in the fingertip moving on the string.

Of course, rhythmic pulsations arising from the music can be reinforced in the right arm unit as well as the left. Pulsing out the rhythm in the bow arm in coordination with the left-hand gesture assists the realization of the total act. In the right arm, with its rich manifestations in movement, the pulse again helps the player in finding balances through movement. Trying to "hold the tone steady" by inhibiting movement is not uncommon, and from this practice comes immobility, then tension, and ul-

---

[4]Havas, *A New Approach to Violin Playing*, p. 30.

timately some form of anxiety. Sensing the rhythmic movement of the music in the bow arm leads to a controlled use of the bow displacement, speed and weight.

ARTICULATION

What gives rise to the different types of bow strokes is, of course, the desire for a variety of articulations of musical ideas. There can be no significant musical value in being able to mechanically perform a type of bowing which has no application in music-making. Like all things, the reason for the different bow strokes must arise from the musical insight. As the music is acted out in the tonal-rhythmic structures gestured in the left hand, the individual notes must have as a distinct element of their character a definite articulation, that is to say, one must imagine exactly the kind of sound that initiates the note and finishes it. The *attack and release* of each note accounting for its articulation will form the general effect of the music when heard in an integrated form. It is the quality of the beginning and ending of each note which must be made evident in the musical concept. When one allows the interval progressions gestured in the left hand to decide the appropriate movements of the bow, then the bow can move in perfect coordination with the musical concept.

The ideal of the New Approach is to allow the cellist to deal with the rhythm of the music as it is expressed in the interval progression. The trigger for this musical activity is the *inner vocalization* of those intervals. When the left-hand gestures carry out the transformation of these ideas, and the bow movement is coordinated with these left-hand gestures, one is simply carrying out the mental command that identifies each note on the basis of its total character—its pitch, duration and dynamic—and the resulting tone quality which is a combination of these three factors.

6 Shifting and Double Stops

THE SHIFT

When the player has made a complete investigation of the intervals that exist in the first and half positions, he should proceed to the learning of the second, third and fourth positions. These positions are more limited in range because there is no open string to assist in the playing of the intervals; however, when two positions are connected by the *shift,* the possibility of using a great variety of interval progressions becomes evident. One must progressively learn the musical potential of the various intervals existing in all the neck positions, for then the entire lower and middle registers of the cello can be used.

It is a common practice to study the fourth position after the first and half positions. With the use of these three positions, a large number of musical passages can be performed without recourse to further change of position. It is essential, however, that third and second position be given their due attention, for each in its own way is highly valuable to the mastery of the neck positions. Facility will be gained by the careful study of music that can be exclusively played in any one given position. The complete knowledge of interval progressions and their resulting form imprints must be gained across all four strings in each position.

Kato Havas has written, "When the student is completely at home in all positions, the actual change from one position to another (provided the base joints [knuckles] are in sole control) creates no problem at all. The preparation of a sideway and vertical action is exactly the same as when going from one note to another in the same position. But when changing from one position to another both the mental and physical preparation are even more exaggerated."[1]

---

[1]Havas, *A New Approach to Violin Playing,* p. 38.

CONTROL OF THE SHIFT

The control of the shift exists in one's ability to accept the sequence of events: vivid conception of the interval, bold command triggering spontaneous movement, and finger preparation with its thrust and release. Many players are hampered by faulty or vague conception of the musical interval. When there is *clarity* of the ideational objective, the command *is* bold, and the triggering device works. If the ideational objective is vague, the command lacks definite direction. Command follows conceptualization. Once the total response is triggered, then the player must allow it to run its course in a pliant way always responsive to the messages streaming in from the points of contact. The sequence of events promotes the best possible conditions for communication of the musical ideas.

The gestures are timed if the musical pulse is felt, and here the pulsing of the music becomes an invaluable device for the physical movements. The judgment of how much time one needs to connect two widely-separated points in sound must depend on musical values, not mechanical ones. Organic architectural interpretation will give to each interval its own timing, and the musical quality of the shifting will enhance the technique.

The strongest possible attraction between the notes is the actual sound of the interval with its musical distance well established in the mind. The actual spatial distance on the fingerboard should not be a primary concern. Even the large physical distances encountered on the cello can be made of secondary importance through proper finger preparation. The cellist must conquer the actual spatial problems by concentrating on the musical design so that real physical distance does not feel extended, but diminished.

TENDENCY   To view the large distance and to feel immobile. The finger presses into the string and creates undue traction in the shift. There is no confident use of the rhythmic pulsation of the music.

SOLUTION   To identify the note consciously, i.e., sing its name (aim with the ear) and shoot the finger into its new position, thrusting it forward from the knuckle. The physical solution for shifting in large intervals lies in utilizing the basic finger preparation skill in a variation which has larger preparation and greater thrust and always moves on the basis of the rhythmic pulse of the music.

The point of contact between the fingertip and the string must be very sensitive and pliant. The least amount of undue traction during the actual shift will frustrate the shifting movement. The player must *poise* his finger on the note which sounds first, *pulse* on the string, *trigger* the new note (sing its name) and *shoot* the finger forward to find its mark. In several cases, such as playing rapidly repeated notes, the *pulsing of the finger* replaces the actual thrust from above the string. This pulsing is transmitted to the fingertip through the mobile joints of the finger.

INTERMEDIARY NOTES

All cellists should learn the function of intermediary notes which assist in the shift by relating the hand to the new position through a guiding finger. This will enhance the acquaintance with that combination of fingers which will produce the most connected quality of movement in the shift. When the player shifts from note to note on any one string with the *same finger* (whether ascending or descending), the shift will have its most connected (legato) quality of movement. When shifting (ascending) from one finger to an adjacent higher-numbered finger, one experiences the next most connected quality of movement, then comes non-consecutive fingers, and finally shifting (ascending) from higher-numbered fingers to lower-numbered fingers. The use of intermediary notes offers a variation in the method of changing to the new finger when playing the notes of a widely-spaced interval. When rapid changes of position take place, the use of the intermediary note is less pronounced.

DESCENDING INTERVALS

When shifting from one position to another, the player must give careful attention to the descending intervals. One must encourage the *forward* action of the new finger (in a plane from scroll toward bridge) just as one does in the case of playing small intervals in-position. One must never press the fingertip into the string and pull the finger backward (toward the scroll) in the descending interval shifts. The cellist must poise the shifting finger, send it forward, and the movement of the entire left arm unit will take the finger to its new note. The fingertip movement from one point of contact to another in the descending interval shift is only a part of a total response. The successful shift depends on the mobility of the entire left arm unit. This mobility is characterized by a freely-moving upper arm, a flexible elbow, a pliant wrist, and a left hand that is responsive to the total cooperation of the limbs and expresses movement that has been initiated far from the fingertip pulsing on the string.

During practice it is worthwhile to take the shifting finger forward (ascend) to a note in the *same position* in order to reinforce this forward action and feel the suppleness of the entire left arm unit. When this forward action has been established, one should sing the name of the note and this triggering device will take the finger successfully to the new pitch. As the release is made, the point of contact between fingertip and string will be conducive to good tone production.

DOUBLE-STOP CATEGORIES

In addition to the double stops which are either perfect fifths or are created by a combination of one stopped note and one open string, the double stops fall into two categories according to the manner in which they are produced physically:

1. Sixths, Sevenths, Octaves.
   These double stops are performed with the lower-numbered finger using the lower of the two strings.

2. Fourths, Thirds, Seconds.
    These double stops are performed with the lower-num-
    bered finger using the higher of the two strings.

When taking the notes of the double stops separately during
practice, the lower-numbered finger in every case should be the
mobile point of balance. When the shape and positioning of the
hand is a *result* of finding the balance on this lower-numbered
finger, then one simply drops the other finger into place. This
avoids the urge to stretch the fingers apart and place them separately. As one hangs on the fingers with a feeling of weight
below, always balancing on the lower-numbered finger, the
double stops will feel secure, and the threat of gripping with the
fingertips will be eliminated. When playing double stops, the
cellist should utilize his skill of finger preparation to new advantage, assuring the thrust and release of all notes involved in
the chord. As he sustains the double stops he should seek freedom
of movement, and must always have a full tactile awareness of
the pliant fingertips pulsing on the strings. When the music demands a shift of the double stops from one position to another,
it is the mobile lower-numbered finger that assumes the responsibility of the balance.

PERFECT FIFTH DOUBLE STOPS

On the cello, the perfect fifth is a problematic double stop.
Because of the width of the fingerboard, it is not possible to keep
the fingertip engaged on two strings at once when playing a
perfect fifth double stop. When this double stop is required, the
finger must be flattened and placed laterally across the strings so
that they are stopped simultaneously by the same finger. In a
slow tempo, when the interval of the perfect fifth is played melo-
dically, the finger can be lifted from the knuckle and dropped
into position on the adjacent string; however, when the tempo
quickens, the finger must be used in the flattened position. While
neither position is particularly difficult in itself, the player must

be able to employ combinations of the two positions of the finger, playing perfect fifths in melodic patterns and double-stop perfect fifths. This forms a unique study for the cellist, and when control is gained in recovering the normal position of the finger following its flattened use, the player can feel at ease with the performance of the perfect fifths.

THIRDS

Of all the various combinations of double stops played in consecutive order in the low positions (without the aid of the thumb position), it is the thirds which are most likely to tax the hand. In playing thirds, the first finger used on the higher string and the fourth finger used on the lower string must be carefully prepared if the player is to avoid undue stretching and downward pressure on the strings. One must remember that the balance of the hand is decided in the positioning of the first finger, which must be very pliant and mobile. The cellist must never *reach* with the fourth finger, but should swing on the first finger and *drop* the fourth finger in place. Careful attention must be given to the left thumb, which is loosely related to the neck of the cello. If the thumb clamps beneath the first finger and the pinching action of the hand is brought into play, the fourth finger will *feel* foreshortened. The player should explore the changing possibilities of the left thumb placement. As in the case of playing single notes, when the player finds comfort and release from tension in double-stop playing, the tone production will immediately become sonorous, and the bow will cling to both vibrating strings, drawing forth a beautiful tone.

INTERVAL CHAINS

The cellist will remember that singing the note's name with the inner musical voice cues the beginning of the gesture, while pulsing the note rhythmically keeps the gesture operative throughout the duration of the tone. The study of interval chains utilizes this learning device. During this type of study the cellist may investigate a variety of interval combinations and their fingering possibilities. Playing interval chains is a progressively staged process that can be expanded to incorporate many aspects of the New Approach training. The cellist must exercise his imaginative use of *variation* in dealing with the daily implementation of this type of study. The following explanations for the use of interval chain studies are based on a typical selection of musical material. One should simply make a random choice of intervals to begin the study.

EXAMPLE NO. I   MAJOR SIXTH—PERFECT FOURTH

Use a descend-ascend movement pattern beginning in the fourth position and utilize the fingering 1-3 in the following manner:

One must vary the effect and stage the development by using different combinations of the interval chain study on alternate practice periods. Always utilize several fingering possibilities, for instance 1-3:1-3, then 2-4:2-4, thus finding the balance on different lower-numbered fingers.

EXAMPLE NO. Ia

Use string crossing for development. Cross between two strings, then three strings and finally all four strings. This will expand the in-position aspects of the interval chain study and will allow for a variety of combinations of in-position and changing position practice.

Example No. II

Example No. IIa

Avoid the tendency to use the interval chain study as a "finger exercise." It must be a study in vocalization. It should change in complexity *only* in relation to the increasing ability to use the cue device. Remember that the inner musical voice sings the note's name, which cues the beginning of the physical gesture, while the consequent monosyllabic singing of the pulsing syllable propels the tone through musical time.

Other combinations of intervals might include Minor Sixth-Augmented Fourth (1-2:1-2). This interval chain utilizes more closely spaced fingers.

Example III

Permutations will arise when several interval chains are combined, as in the case of Major Sixth-Perfect Fourth-Minor Sixth-Augmented Fourth (1-3:1-3:1-2:1-2 or 2-4:2-4:2-3:2-3).

Example IIIa

The cellist should also utilize the higher numbered fingers with interval chains, such as the Minor Sixth-Augmented Fourth (3-4:3-4).

Example No. IIIb

Widely spaced intervals form even other possibilities and utilize widely spaced fingers.

Example IV

Minor Seventh—Major Third (1-4:1-4)

Major Seventh—Minor Third (1-4:1-4)

Another developing feature in the interval chain study is the expanded use of the shifting possibility. This aspect must be progressively staged. One begins with the chromatic semitone shift as seen in the preceding examples, then uses the whole tone shift, then the larger intervalic shifts, at which time the combinations of intervals created by the shifting give new permutations to the study.

Example V

Double stopping the interval chain study is another important aspect. One should begin with simple double stops utilizing two strings, then progressively use three strings and finally all four strings. When performing double stop interval chains vocalize the note played by the lower-numbered finger to assist finding the balance of the hand.

Example VI

The use of interval chains of widely-spaced combinations is valuable. These interval chains performed with rhythmic variants and various articulations should be an outgrowth of the entire study.

Example VII

Various articulations should be spontaneously designed during the course of the daily study of interval chains. All examples have been shown with simple détaché; however, all bowings are useful, and the numerous legato bowings will lead to the sustained tone.

Example VIII

The cellist should not seek speed when implementing the cue device. Until the cue device becomes totally interiorized, the danger of its use fading in favor of concentration on the particulars of the physical action is great.

Several examples are given here for different articulations arising from the accentuated détaché.

Example IX

Martelé (in upper half of the bow)

Example X

Thrown Spiccato (at the balance point of the bow)

In the spiccato practice reduce the frequency of the string crossing by increasing the repetition of the pitch.

Example XI

Springing Spiccato (involuntary)

Example XII

Firm Staccato

First use a *pointillistic* device, both down and up bow. Gradually remove the rhythmic silences to produce the firm staccato articulation.

Shifting interval chains *on one string* will prove valuable but should be preceded by a preparatory study during which the cellist performs scales on one string using each finger alternately throughout an entire octave. These scales should be played on all four strings. Begin by repeating each pitch (down bow—up bow). When the scales can be played fluently with one finger, the cellist should proceed with the shifting interval chains on one string.

Example XIII

Triads and various forms of Thirds

Perfect Fourths

Perfect Fifths resolved

Minor and Major Sixths resolved

Minor and Major Sevenths resolved

Example XIV

Compound Intervals

7 Summary

MUSICAL IDEATION

When formulating the principles of the New Approach, Kato Havas integrated certain elements into a new form and produced a working system based on the utilization of the naturally-evolving fundamental balances. This new order depends on the recreation of a musical design perceived by the mind. When the logic of this thought process is accepted, the cellist dealing with New Approach principles will begin to search for a technique—a feeling for the instrument—which is entirely in the service of music-making. The first consideration is the sequence of events upon which the New Approach depends.

The match/mismatch processes operate continuously during the hours spent practicing. The cellist must have an organized effort in order to set his musical goals and give direction to the practice. It is of critical importance that this organization is directed at the appropriate aspect of the sequence of events. First comes the clarity of musical idea and the setting of the end-result goals. New practice incentives will arise from increased perceptual sensitivity and depth of musical insight. Certain "problems" will simply solve themselves when the cellist becomes convinced that he will not sacrifice his ideational capacities by allowing the mind to direct consciously what the body is prepared to do automatically.

Simple and bold devices related to the musical concepts will trigger the automatic physical responses. These gestures of cello playing will be carried out by the nervous system without the direction of the mind. If the ideas are sharp and clear, if the cue devices are effective, and if the postural aspects of the body are in a natural state, the transformation will be complete. Musical ideas will be translated into tonal realities with artistic and communicative value. During the practice, one is fulfilled by the constant realization that the end-result idea is being matched by physical reality as the cello-playing movements evolve naturally. The cellist becomes a transmitter of music.

One must never neglect or deny the existence of the ideation that gives purpose to the triggering devices. The whole thing is an ideokinetic complex born in the mind only when the player sits poised and ready to play. The entire event is planned before the bow is drawn. This rough plan is constantly adjusted in accord with the information that streams back from the points of contact. Only two things are necessary: one is that the "command" is indeed ideokinetic, and the other is that one "lets it happen naturally"—that is, lets the total response evolve through the body which is in its most natural state. All this will happen if the cellist knows where to direct his explicit focal attention.

NATURE OF TECHNIQUE

The very nature of the cello and its characteristic music establishes the task of our technique. Our most usual technical concern is the performance of a single line, a progression of musical intervals. This basic enterprise has given reason for the cellistic technique to exist as it does in a sequence of events which begins with the concept of the end-result desired, continues with automatic physical movement, and terminates with the production of sound *per se*.

Once the musical objective is sharp and clear and the body is in a state of readiness to act, the program required for its realization is triggered. The automatic physical movements—the gestures of cello playing—are organized subcortically, and the movement pattern evolves or "happens" if one allows it to do so. Cello technique is not a mere repertoire of segmented body movements. It is a total mental-physical adjustment to the music and the instrument. It is characteristic that the process of acquiring such a technique is concurrent with the growth of musical insight.

IMAGINATION

Imagination plays an important role in the life of the performing musician. It should be the tool used constantly by every recreative performer. It is through the use of imaginative musical concepts that the cellist sets goal-images upon which his body can act spontaneously. The goal-images are created as the performer lives through a creative learning experience and habituates certain physical skills through practice. The imaginative use of these musical concepts is the key to artistry and communicative performance. The goal-images the cellist sets are created from his sensory memory both past and contemporary. Without ample goal-images based on the perceptions yoked to cello playing, the cellist will encounter difficulties during the performing process as his explicit focal attention can easily become fixed on the physical manipulation of the cello rather than on the musical concepts to be transformed into sound.

Becoming aware of what is *happening at the moment* and responding *only* to that awareness has wonderful results. Many times, if one does not react to the present with definite conviction, one may instead respond to some past situation, some memory habit. One must not try to exist in the promise of a future performance, or the memory of a past one. The cellist must form the habit of being totally involved in the present moment. The mind must focus on the temporal aspect of the musical design, and the body must be constantly regulated by the information resulting from its sensory perception.

UNIFIED SKILLS

Another cause of confusion and the resulting feelings of nervousness and anxiety is the habit of trying to do many things at one time. The feelings are put aside when the player keeps his mind off the details of the physical acts evolving and directs the musical happening. One cannot control movement cortically and at the same time concern the mind with musical content. Unification of the diverse aspects of technique will help us convince ourselves and use a thought process that allows us to concentrate our full awareness, all our responsiveness on the *one thing*—translating musical ideas into sound. When we work with this attitude we are free from the feelings of hurry and anxiety. We are not insisting on doing *consciously* what can be done *automatically*.

That the mind selects and organizes and gives shape to what we hear inwardly is the foundation of all musical organization and the clue to expressive possibilities of musical performance. One must train the inner musical voice so that the concepts generated program the composer's creation when translated into sound. It is this "voice" or memory of musical structure that often falters under the stress of performance. For the performing cellist, there must be an immense collection of information stored in the mind and within easy access through this inner musical voice.

As the mind perceives the interval, it is identified by the memory of its characteristic personality. It is at this stage that the cellist can use his knowledge—perceptual and conceptual—to great benefit. The inner musical voice must reveal the interval to the body. When the command (the singing of the note-name that sets the body into motion) is given, this triggering device is based on a rich conceptual fabric that one wants reproduced in the tones emitted from the cello.

The interval progression as it is revealed by the inner musical voice is not an abstraction, but has the personality bestowed upon it by its tacit dimension, that is, the combination of perceptual sensitivity plus training. The musical qualities which are understood and revealed by this voice are, in fact, the goal which our physical movement will convert into sound. The premise is that the IDENTITY OF THE NOTES AND THE "FEEL" OF THEIR PERFORMANCE BY THE CELLIST ON HIS INSTRUMENT ARE UNIFIED. They become the end-result of our intentions. This is unification in technique.

THE NATURAL BALANCES

The natural balances are known to everyone from their constant use in rudimentary movement. What must be learned is how to apply them to cello playing. During infancy we begin to enjoy our physical ability to carry out certain goals in movement. At

this time, one discovers that certain movements controlled through the balances are appropriate to achieving certain goals. A child does not begin to learn to walk by being consciously concerned with the action of his toes, but walks moving the legs from the hips. The smaller, more subtle movements are cultivated and refined as the skill is practiced through goal seeking, and walking finally happens involuntarily, not by a conscious will to control each segmented movement. Luckily, most people become "natural" walkers, and go about the business of walking with a certain mental-physical abandon. As the newly-found prowess is trusted, and one proceeds with confidence in the seeking of goals through movement, *form is born from function,* conscious effort is put aside, and spontaneous movement is used to improvise and vary the basic skill.

The so-called "natural" cello player, like the "natural" walker, has removed certain mental-physical obstacles and simply "lets it happen." The principles of the New Approach can be used immediately and with observable musical results by every player, whether he is a beginner or an advanced player. On the basis of his own physique and mentality, each player will take the application to a different level of achievement according to his imaginative use of the ideas.

Because the ideas lend themselves to a seemingly unlimited use and due to the rather recent formulation of the New Approach, its potential has not been fully brought to light. Much lies ahead for the player willing to examine and apply these principles to cello playing. In this new order dwells the promise of the cellist as an instrument of expression, a transmitter of music.

References and Selected Readings

Alexander, F. Matthias. *The Use of the Self.* New York: E. P. Dutton and Co., Inc., 1932.

————. *The Universal Constant in Living.* New York: E. P. Dutton and Co., Inc., 1941.

Alexanian, Diran. *Traité théorique et pratique du violoncelle.* Paris: Editions Salabert, 1922.

Bonpensiere, Luigi. *New Pathways to Piano Technique.* New York: Philosophical Library, 1953.

Duport, Jean Louis. *Essai sur le Doigté du Violoncelle.* Paris, 1819.

Dounis, D. C. *The Artist's Technique of Violin Playing.* New York: Carl Fischer, Inc., n.d.

Eisenberg, Maurice. *Cello Playing Today.* London: The Strad, 1957.

Gruppe, Paulo M. *A Reasonable and Practical Approach to the Cello.* Published by the Author, 1964.

Gunn, John. *The Theory and Practice of Fingering the Violoncello.* London, 1793.

Havas, Kato. *A New Approach to Violin Playing.* London: Bosworth and Co., Ltd., 1961.

————. *The Twelve Lesson Course in a New Approach to Violin Playing.* London: Bosworth and Co., Ltd., 1964.

————. *The Violin and I, An Autobiographical Account with the Controversial Correspondence on the New Approach.* London: Bosworth and Co., Ltd., 1968.

————. *Stage Fright.* London: Bosworth and Co., Ltd., 1973.

Hellebrandt, F. A. "The New Approach to Violin Playing." *The Strad,* 80 (1969), 277-281, 305-311, 361-365.

————. "The Role of the Thumb in the New Approach to Violin Playing." *The Strad,* 80 (1970), 421-431.

————. "The Role of the Mind in the New Approach to Violin Playing." *The Strad,* 80 (1970), 473-479.

————. "Project Evaluation (Chapter Nine)." *Final Report, Project No. 5-1182,* U.S. Department of Health, Education, and Welfare, Office of Education, Bureau of Research.

Leland, Valborg. *The Dounis Principles of Violin Playing.* London: The Strad, 1949.

Polanyi, Michael. *The Tacit Dimension.* New York: Doubleday and Company, Inc., 1966.

Zuckerkandl, Victor. *Sound and Symbol, Music and the External World.* Princeton: University Press, 1969.